Journey

to

Joy

A GUIDE TO FINDING PEACE, HAPPINESS AND PURPOSE

Celia Sankar

Damascus Press

Published in 2002 by
Damascus Press
Suite 201, 95 Hutchison Avenue
Elliot Lake, ON P5A 1W9
Canada

Portions of this book can be found at:
www.celiasankar.com
E-mail:
info@celiasankar.com

Canadian Cataloguing in Publication Data

Sankar, Celia, 1970-
Journey to joy: a guide to finding
peace, happiness and purpose

ISBN 0-9689109-1-2
1. Self-realization.
I. Title.
BL624.S26 2002   158.1   C2001-903464-4

Printed and bound in Canada

What readers are saying about *"Journey to Joy"*

"Sankar shows the process that unlocks the truths which can take us out of darkness into the light of joy."
—**Barbara Lewis-Marco**, Author, *Stumbling Toward Enlightenment, An Illustrated Crisis Companion*

"Despairing and down on your luck? Try Sankar's pluck for a pick-me-up. Sankar invites, encourages and directly inspires readers to use her journal as a pathway home to the heart and soul of themselves."
—**Suzanne Grenager**, Life Coach and Columnist

"This is a book you can pick up anytime and no matter if you read one small section or a few pages, it is full of richness and encouragement on our daily journey to know ourselves and our loving God."
—**Sister Diane Guertin**, Hospital Pastoral Care Director

"For the person looking for support after a negative experience, the author offers a tool-kit for a journey in self-discovery: a return to a self-confident image, anticipating the future and its opportunities for a joyful life."
—**Barbara Fazekas**, Librarian

"Sankar offers us enlightenment, a worthwhile challenge and a realm of new possibilities. The book opened up for me an opportunity to look deeper within, to seek congruity in all parts of my life and to continue to strive to be honest with myself."
—**Daniel Robitaille**, High School Teacher

About the Author

Celia Sankar is an internationally acclaimed journalist and writer who has reported from Europe, Asia, the Middle East, South America and the Caribbean, as well as from remote areas and major cities of the United States and Canada. She has worked with *The Globe and Mail*, *The Vancouver Sun*, *The Victoria Times-Colonist*, *The Times* of London and the *Sunday Times* of London, and is a former associate editor of the *Trinidad Express*, one of the Caribbean's leading dailies.

The winner of several international media awards, Sankar did her Master's in journalism in London, England, on a Commonwealth Press Union Fellowship, and teaches writing at an Ontario college. She has been a life-long seeker of truth and student of wholesome living. Through her inspirational newspaper columns, lectures and an inspirational radio talk-show which she co-hosted, Sankar has touched the lives of thousands in many parts of the world.

This book is dedicated to my dear parents,
Jeff and Claudette, and to my precious sister and brothers,
Lisa, Simon and Stanley. I feel greatly blessed to have
started my life in your company.

Acknowledgement

No man — or woman — is an island. That saying became powerfully evident as I prepared this book for publication. I could not have completed this project without the love, support and encouragement of a great many people who gave freely of their time and of themselves.

I would like to acknowledge and say thank you to all those who read and commented on early versions of the manuscript, including persons mentioned elsewhere in this book, and others, such as my great friend and former editor Lennox Grant, author Nina Atwood, Fr. Andre Lemieux, Rev. Jody Medicoff, Lucille Gauthier, Rose Tomic, Barbara Torrance and Martine Hillis. I owe a great debt of gratitude to my sister Lisa and brother-in-law Zhu Wei for their enormous contribution to the final preparatory work on this project. I am grateful to Mr Li and Madam Jiang for the boost to my determination to see this endeavor through. I say thanks to my father for his unwavering belief in me and a huge thank you to my mother for the day-to-day support which made it possible for me to dedicate myself to this work. Above all, I acknowledge and give thanks to God for enabling me to walk on this path.

Contents

Introduction

From Paris to Vancouver, from Iowa City to Tel Aviv and Beijing, everywhere I have traveled, I have found a common underlying theme in the ambitions of the people I have met. No matter a person's color or mother-tongue or situation in life, we all speak the same language when it comes to our most cherished desire.

Basically, we all want to be happy.

We want to provide well for ourselves and our loved ones. We want to be able to laugh and retain that good feeling throughout the day. We want to feel at peace with ourselves, comfortable within our skin. We would like to put our hands to work on something and feel proud about the successful results. We would like other people to think well of us, and to love us. We also want these good things for the people we care for, our family and friends.

A life of joy is the universal human goal. Unfortunately, many never achieve it.

For many, life is an eternal struggle. They awake every morning with a sigh. They are reluctant to get out of bed and face whatever lies ahead. That may be overwhelming tears, fear, anger, shame, boredom, stress, lack, frustration, and strife at home, at work and every place in between. For these people, each day ends with a joyless sigh that they have made it through their waking hours without losing their sanity.

What a tragedy that is. How sad it is to slug through life and never know how full of passion and rich with pleasure each day can be.

Life presents a door to a better way

When we live life in this manner, at some point the burden of such a weary existence becomes too much.

At that time, we feel a deep, intense unhappiness. This pain often comes acutely after a traumatic event (such as the death of a loved one, the end of a marriage or a relationship, the loss of a promotion, the failure of a business venture), or it is chronic in a life that seems hollow and unfulfilling.

It is here we find a wonderful paradox: the anguish we suffer in such a situation, this grief which we wish we never faced, can turn out to be the very best thing that could ever happen to us. For it is this pain that forces us into ourselves. We go deep inside, and if we open ourselves to the lessons of the moment, we emerge stronger, wiser, and, yes, happier.

The distressing moment presents us with a door to a better way of living.

When our world has fallen apart or when we are in the midst of turmoil, it may seem as if a better future could not possibly exist. The truth, however, is that joy is readily available; it only awaits our claiming it.

If you are at a point of crisis in your life, this book is meant to give you comfort and to inspire you to make it through this stage. It shares the message of hope that you can conquer whatever ails you right now. Further, it offers a proven program, based on universal and eternal principles of successful living, that can help you transform your life.

A persistent feeling of unhappiness is commonly the result of fear, anger, shame, self-hate and a range of other thoughts and feelings that sap us of enthusiasm for life. Often we are not even aware we are chained down by these negative forces.

Freedom from such debilitating thoughts and feelings is easily within reach. The power to claim that freedom is nestled right inside us. *Know that you already have that power.*

If you feel dissatisfied or disappointed with your life right now, you simply have to learn ways to exercise that power in order to create an existence that is beautiful and rewarding.

A personal passage

Although as a journalist I have, over the years, interviewed hundreds of people (including researchers, psychologists, therapists and religious leaders) in order to discover what makes for a happy existence, I write to share these assurances with you not as any expert, but simply as a fellow traveler on the journey of life.

I know because I have walked this road myself.

I know what it feels like to live through intense emotional pain that takes over and shuts down your life. I know, too, the relief, the joy and the sense of power and possibility that is your reward when you march out of that troubled section of your journey in this world.

This book came about during a period when I experienced the unhappy coincidence of a number of difficult circumstances: the bitter end of a relationship, a tough career change, feeling isolated from my family in a small town in a foreign country, and a major schism in my family.

I felt life had knocked the wind out of me and I couldn't get back up. For days, I would lie on my bed, paralyzed by the thought that my life was as a wreck. I felt all chances for love, children, financial success, recognition, peace and happiness had been cruelly ripped away from me. I would swing from crying and wanting to end my life to boiling with a fierce rage. These thoughts were so powerful and the feelings were so intense, I became terrified of myself.

I knew this was no way to live. I felt I was sinking and it was only a matter of time before I would go under completely. It was in my most wretched moments that I realized I needed divine help to get me to sure ground. I had to open up my soul to receive inspiration. That was when I began to rise in the purity and quiet before dawn to write messages to revive myself. I never planned what to write. I would pick up my pen and let the words flow. It is these messages, revised slightly for publication, that I share with you in this book.

These writings, which tapped my many years of truth-seeking at a time when I needed it most, showed me how to start living again. They took me from feeling totally lost to creating a new life of joy. As I applied the principles contained in this book, my world began to open up. New opportunities presented themselves before me, including the challenge of lecturing at college level. I began a more rewarding phase in my writing career. I started my own business. I saw my income increase seven-fold and I paid off my mortgage. I opened myself to a more fulfilling relationship and the troubles in my family ceased to be a worry.

I am in the best place I have been all my life. Now, each day when I awake, I jump out of bed with a prayer of thanks. I feel privileged, as if God has given me a second chance to live. Actually, no, what I truly feel is that for the first time, I am truly living. My life today is filled with peace and gratitude, and my days are fuelled by purpose. And when the blues threaten to return, because they do and always will, I know where to turn for support.

Self-love is the key

It is because I know how frightened, lost and alone one can feel while stumbling along the rocky path that I have published this book. Originally, I wrote it for my spirit only. Over the last couple of years, however, I have shared it with an ever-widening circle of many of my family, friends and their friends and acquaintances, and I have been gratified and amazed to see their enthusiastic response. Many have reported feeling refreshed and invigorated by these writings.

Now, I share it with you because during my own struggles, I searched for and found little that could guide me step by step into happier times. I came across many wonderful books which correctly said self-love was key to living happily, but which did not show what exactly one needed to do to conquer the pain of daily misery. This book seeks to fill that gap.

These meditations and affirmations comprise a program

to enable you to master the thoughts and feelings in your life and, therefore, create the joyful existence you desire.

Through my own experience and after years of research on personal growth and recovery from life's traumas, it is clear to me that our greatest handicap in experiencing joy is what I will call a crisis of the self. Our deepest sorrow strikes when an unformed "self" or a flawed concept of "self" is forced by circumstances to confront its incompleteness or its flaw. The truth of the state of the self is unacceptable to the individual. That truth is so painful to face that the individual's systems shut down, either totally, rendering the person incapable of functioning in society, or partially, with the person experiencing life in limbo.

I now consider that pain a gift, for it wakes us up. It presents right before our eyes problems that have been lurking unattended. It gives us the opportunity to fix whatever needs to be corrected if we are to lead fuller, richer lives.

In my own case, my painful experience taught me that I was an unformed "self". I had no concept of a separate "me" that existed in the world. My identity was as part of my family, and, later, as part of a couple.

Through this painful period of my life, I also realized that what little sense of self I had was flawed: my identity was wrapped up in my work, and when my efforts proved less successful than before, I crumbled. I have learnt that it is wholly possible to be an achiever, to have pride in one's accomplishments and still lack self-confidence; pride in one's achievements and self-confidence are not the same thing. You can have self-confidence or self-esteem only if you know yourself.

This experience has taught me to discover and enjoy my individuality. It has taught me that work — even the most fulfilling work — is something you do, not who you are. I now know that it is my lifelong duty to myself to know, nurture, preserve and honor my "self".

Knowing, understanding and loving who you are works like magic in your life. It is the key that opens a door to a bright, beautiful world. It is an awakening that pervades every aspect of your life. It guides all your decisions and actions. Suddenly, you find yourself recognizing and avoiding situations that would cause you pain. And almost instinctively, you begin to gravitate to and create situations that would bring you joy.

How to use this book

If you are facing your toughest battle yet in life, I sincerely hope that you find strength and inspiration within these pages.

Here, you will find meditations, motivational messages, affirmations and directions for exercises that can help you discover, understand and love the wonderful person that you are. Further, you will find passages that can inspire you to determine how best to care for your "self" and how to live happily with others in this world.

There are two ways you can approach this book that would be helpful. You may choose to read it objectively, that is, as a person observing and learning from someone else's struggles. Psychology researchers say watching others and then adapting those observations to ourselves is the most effective way of learning behavior; it is, after all, how we acquired much of our personality traits as children.

The second way you may approach this book is to read it subjectively. That is to say, where you find you relate deeply to the messages, adopt them, read them as affirmations and encouragement to yourself. Feel free to scratch out parts that don't apply to you; in the margins and blank spaces, write thoughts and situations that reflect your life; underline, highlight and bookmark those parts that touch you most profoundly.

Whatever approach you take, I suggest you get a journal and write your own messages to yourself. You know your life story, your fears, your hurts, your dreams. The messages you write, following the pattern of those in this book, will be deeply personal and will speak to your innermost being. A good time to do such writing is in the quiet of the early morning, before your mind and soul are troubled with the many battles that make up daily life.

I also suggest you take this book with you wherever you go. Whenever you feel you need it, whip it out to give yourself a boost.

Reading this book once is not enough. Repetition is the key to learning, and so I suggest you re-read these messages several times. I find strength and inspiration in these words even today. I have discovered that by the very act of reading inspirational thoughts and motivational messages such as these, we set the stage for serenity and joy to enter our lives.

I will warn you, though, if you are expecting this book to work for you, that is, if you expect this book of itself to bring bliss into your life, you will be disappointed. This book will not work for you. There is no book that has ever been written which will work for you. No retreat and no healing workshop will work for you. The only way you will make it out of dark days into happier times is if *you* work with this book or any other book or retreat or workshop. *You are always the most crucial part of the equation.*

Think of this book as a tool-kit. The material here can help you restore your life. Think of it in this way: let's say you decide to renovate your kitchen and you purchase a tool-kit and bring it home. The tool-kit is worthless unless you use it. You can not look at the hammer and the drill and expect them to build cupboards for you. You have to pick them up and do the job. So, too, you can not read these words and expect the book to bring joy into your life. You have to take these words and use them, live by them.

It takes courage to make it through your darkest hour to a time of new joy. It takes you — your presence, your determination, your sincerity. By picking up this book, you have shown you want to be there. Just follow through by living by these messages and those you write to inspire yourself. When you do, believe me, the daybreak will shortly come. And trust me even more on this, it will be the most beautiful time of your life.

Create your circle of strength

Society is not structured to nurture and support the person going through his or her painful passage. The world hardly cares to know you in your moment of defeat. It's not glamorous; it's not sexy. The cameras flash and the crowds cheer for the moments of glory, and so people shout about their triumphs, but conceal their seasons of loss. So, when we feel lost, we often feel alone; we fear something must be wrong with us because we wrongly believe others never go through this too.

I now strongly believe we owe it to ourselves and to each other to share those moments of pain and loss — when time has made us ready to do so. In sharing our experiences, we free ourselves from the prison called "keeping up appearances"; we relieve ourselves of the burden of pretending we are always strong or our lives are perfect. We let ourselves be known as the humans we are, with all the beauty and limitations the term implies.

If you are stumbling along the rocky path, there is no need to be ashamed of what you are going through. Know that this is simply a passage, and that rich rewards await you when you navigate your way through.

The absurd notion that it is shameful adds an unnecessary burden to your task and hinders you in moving forward. Cast it off; banish shame. If pain is now or has been part of your experience of living, then so be it. You are like millions of others in suffering for a spell, and like millions of us, when you pull through, you will appreciate the totality of your experiences.

As you create the life of joy you want, it is crucial that you surround yourself with people who can motivate and support you.

There may be people you know who may want to encourage you to focus on what is wrong in your life, just as they want to whimper about what's awful about theirs. Steer clear of such circles of weakness; they will keep you stuck in misery.

Build, instead, circles of strength as you move to higher levels of aliveness. Align yourself with people on the same wavelength, maybe family and friends with whom you share this book and your thoughts, new friends you make at healing workshops, whatever. With a network of fellow travelers, you will find sympathetic ears, shoulders to lean on, helpful advice, understanding and encouragement. And you will find yourself in the deeply rewarding position of being able to share these with others.

I wish you well on your journey. Please let me know of your experiences. I'd like to share them with others so they, too, can benefit from the wisdom and strength you have gleaned along your way. You may write me at the address on the second-to-last page of this book.

Good luck and God bless.

— *Celia Sankar*

The

Solitary

Journey

———————

I am facing a rough time in my life. All around me, the way seems blocked. I feel as if my world has crumbled in on my head, and in the midst of the rubble of my life, the entire universe seems gloomy and pointless.

I will stop right there. I will stop magnifying my troubles. I will stop seeing them as all-powerful and all-encompassing. Stop giving them victory over me.

I know this above all else: I can conquer every difficulty that comes my way. I have the power within me to defeat any force that threatens my enjoyment of life. I shall overcome all obstacles in my way.

Most of the emotional pain I have ever experienced has been because of some form of loss — the loss of a person through death or that person closing up on me, or one of us having to relocate; the loss of something tangible, such as a house, money, a scholarship, a job, a business; the loss of something intangible, likc good health, prestige, faith, confidence in beauty or youth, a sense of security.

Loss is galling because it means life has ripped away from me something I counted on having as part of my future: a certain partner, a certain lifestyle, good health, prestige. This causes undeniable discomforts and creates burdens I did not expect to have to bear. A second and often unacknowledged source of pain is the effect the loss has on my outlook. It shakes my belief that I will ever have satisfaction in life. It makes me fear joy, comfort and security are forever out of reach. When I acknowledge this second, *unfounded* source of pain, I am in a better position to heal myself.

When I am confronted with a deeply painful situation, I rush to protect myself from the hurt. Unfortunately, the methods I often use to deal with the damage exacerbate matters. One of my first reflexes is to deny the loss. The ugly truth may be breathing right into my face, but I refuse to acknowledge it. People around me may warn me of what is happening, I may see glaring signs that things are crumbling around me, and yet I choose to tell myself that it simply isn't so. I make-believe that everything is or soon will be all right and that what I expected will indeed come to pass.

There are those who say the denial response is natural, even necessary, in that it protects you from too hard a blow from the initial shock of your loss. That may be true, but prolonged denial is unhealthy. The longer I refuse to admit what I hoped for is not to be, the longer I stretch out the pain I have to endure.

Often, not only do I deny a lost cause, I go
further to try to revive one which is dead.
This only serves to magnify my pain.
Fighting in vain is the most desperate and
unrewarding action anyone can take. My
efforts only demonstrate how hopeless the
battle is. That very disappointment causes me
to fight even harder, and the vicious cycle
drags me into a vortex of more suffering.

I would do myself the greatest favor by
simply stopping. Stop denying the loss. Stop
fighting the lost battle. Stand still and accept
what is.

When things go wrong, when I have suffered loss, I will allow myself time to grieve. I won't bury the pain somewhere just because people expect me to keep a brave face. I will confront it instead of running away from it.

Pain is a part of life. It is as legitimate as joy or peace. It is not shameful. Crying and withdrawing into myself are two reactions to pain. And if I feel pain, I will allow myself to express it.

But life goes on. Life is change. Joys come and joys go. Peaceful moments come and peaceful moments go. I will let it be so, too, with my pain and my grieving. I will let them be part of my life for a reasonable time, and then let them go.

For how many days, weeks, or months is it reasonable to grieve a loss? It would be silly to try to fix a time frame within which everybody should be done with grieving. The mourning period should be long enough to wash away the hurt and that depends on each person and each situation.

If I am honest with myself, I will realize when I am picking my wounds to prevent them from healing. I will know when I am suckling my grief because I have become comfortable with the feeling and because I am too scared to walk away from it and start again.

How do you move on in life after a painful loss has knocked the wind out of you? What exactly do I do to reach that point where I am no longer denying the loss or fighting to revive what is dead?

The only way is to confront my loss and my pain.

I need to see that which I have lost. Picture it in all its glory. See my grand expectations of it. Now contrast that with the undeniable facts of the present. In this way, I will cut through unhelpful thinking that is ruled by emotions. I will see reality.

The only way to free myself from my pain and loss is to embrace reality. I admit to myself the reality is I no longer have what I had and I will not have what I had hoped for.

I will speak to myself about this loss. I will look into the mirror, look straight into my eyes and admit the situation that is causing me pain. I will write it down and let the cold facts of reality stare back at me from my journal. I will talk about it with someone I can trust.

I will get the words out. I will get the pain out so it can no longer hide inside and cripple me. I will get the reality out so I can no longer hide from it.

I will surrender to reality, how ever painful that may be. I have lost. My expectations have crashed. It's a done deal. I can't erase the past. *I will move on to better things in the future*, but at this present moment, I have lost. I'll say it out loud, again and again: "I surrender to reality."

As I stop denying and fighting reality, I find myself on steadier ground. Denying and fighting are efforts to run away from the pain, and those efforts are fuelled by fear. As I accept and surrender, I realize that the fear of confronting the pain makes it seem much worse than it actually is. No pain and no loss is too great for me to overcome.

On my journey to healing, I am confronting my humanness. It is a scary thing to discover as my training has been to deny or push aside that aspect of myself. I feel weak, sad, hysterical, angry and a whole range of emotions that other people label inappropriate. I face other people's judgment, even in my private moments, because I impose their judgment on myself. And so I stifle my true feelings. They get buried somewhere inside where they remain like a knot waiting to be untied.

Why do I resist letting my emotions run their course? It is because from early on I was fed messages that I should be strong. Boys in particular face this, but girls, too, are told that big girls don't cry. I was told to swallow my anger and to laugh only when it's okay by the rules set by those around me.

All these messages have their usefulness. They have their time and place, but not in my private moment of pain. During a period of self-transforming crisis, I owe it to myself to be the full human that I am. Part of being human is having emotions and reactions that others call weak or inappropriate: I feel afraid, I want to cry, I want to laugh at something that's dreadful. Well, I will go ahead and do it. Feel fully. Acknowledge and give place to my distress without judging myself or restraining myself.

Surrendering to and admitting my loss are the start of releasing myself from the hurt so I can move on. When I surrender to the loss, I expose myself to the full brunt of the pain. I will let this pain and the gamut of emotions it brings course through me. I will let whatever is happening flow through my life. If I do not open up the sluice gate of my emotions, I will be setting up a dam that I will carry around with me. I can already feel it rising, building. At some point, it will burst and I will be faced with a flood that will be more difficult to handle than the challenge I have now.

As I let the emotions run their course, I know they will eventually run out of steam. I have gone on for days, weeks and months crying and beating up on pillows. But I will be patient with myself. I will let this happen. As I honestly let the emotions out, they will come to their natural end. Already, as the days go by, I feel the need to cry less and less. The time will come when I will have no more tears. As I work out the anger, I find myself feeling lighter. I know the time will come when I won't even think of striking that pillow anymore. It will no longer be necessary.

You grow little by little. You heal molecule by molecule. The process takes time. I will allow time to wash over me. I will live and be grateful for each step. I will look forward to progress without anxiety. Anxiety is a poison that does nothing to bring my desires into being. It only sours my present. I won't rush the next stage. It will come. Let me experience the joy of the process itself, of climbing each rung of the ladder towards healing and growth.

It is good to sit and remember. I think back on where I have come from. Without bitterness, I relive the past hurts and triumphs, the glories and defeats. I see how I have been beaten and how I have battled. And I draw strength from it. Hey, I have done all right. I have survived thus far.

The worse the pain I have endured and the more humiliating the suffering I have lived through, the greater the victory it is that I am here today to look back on it all.

When I take a long view of life, I am grateful for my hour of pain. The good times are wonderful; they make life sweet. But it is the turmoil, not the laughter, that forces me into myself. It is when I struggle through a storm, not when I am simply sailing along, that I stretch myself and grow. It is the wretched times that take me to a special place; the times of struggle bring me to the fundamental understanding that I am an individual — one person, alone, separate and apart from every other human being on earth. These rough times are allowing me to discover and appreciate that person.

I realize now that I have walked all my life with a fear of being alone forever. I have been terrified by the thought of growing old in an apartment by myself, with no one to talk to, no one to complain to about aches and pains, no one to call the doctor for me. That fear has not been at the forefront of my mind every day, and I don't have escape from a solitary old age as the motive in my head when I find myself drawn to an attractive stranger. But that deep-seated fear of being alone has always been with me. In forming romantic connections, I am attempting early on in life to avoid a lonely exit from this world.

What does it mean to be lonely? It means to not know myself, for if I know and love myself I will never suffer the devastating pain called loneliness. I am always with me.

I will be in a relationship with myself. I will be kind and gentle with myself. I will bestow on myself the kind of attention and love I know I deserve. I won't wait for or depend on someone else to make me feel worthy of love. I won't delegate to others the job of making me feel special and wonderful. If I do, I will always be a craving, desperate soul.

In practical ways, I will be to myself what I want a life mate to be to me: I will take care of my own financial affairs, treat myself to my favorite meals, get myself a present every once in a while. I will be there for myself emotionally: compliment myself on my looks, praise myself on my accomplishments, accept me for who I am. I will love, honor and cherish myself.

I will love that special person in my life: me.
For in reality, I am the only life mate I will
ever have. Someone else may join me and be
by my side for the journey. What a joy and
privilege it is to have a co-traveler. But that
person may at any moment disappear from
my side through death or a parting of ways.
When I love myself, I will be able to walk
my journey with joy and strength — with or
without a co-traveler.

Journey

to

Selfhood

———

All I am and all I will ever be is this collection of muscles and bones with which I walk this earth; the capacity for emotions and thought with which I interact with the world; and that inner spirit, that piece of God which lives inside me. This is all with which I came into the world. This is all that I will take to the grave.

When life beats me down, when all my dreams have crashed, my "me" is still there. Outside circumstances do not make me any less than I am.

When things go well, yes, even in the midst of success, fame and fortune, my "me" is still there, in its simplicity and nakedness. Outside circumstances do not make me any more than I am.

I need to get to know my "me". I will take
the same amount of time and make the same
effort to get to know myself that I would
dedicate to a stranger with whom I might like
to share my life. I am getting to know my
body. I look at myself in the mirror. I am
enjoying examining every inch of my body. I
am getting acquainted with every scar, every
birthmark, every lump. This is *my* body. It is
not my parents', my future spouse's, nor my
yet-to-be-born children's body. The only
person it belongs to is me. Howsoever it is
today, I accept my body. Accepting it simply
means I acknowledge this is the reality of
how my body is. There are things about it I
would like to change — I want to put on
weight, firm up my thighs and buttocks, get
rid of those scars from childhood — but that
is for tomorrow. Today, I examine, see, really
see, and accept this body with which I am
experiencing life. It is my duty to always
honor, cherish and take care of it. No one
can do that job but me.

I am getting to know my personal story. As I write it down, I am rediscovering my world and the forces and events that have shaped me. I find it silly that I never realized I could or should pay attention to my own history, just as I would devour the details of the life story of a celebrity.

All that I have experienced before goes together to form me. Even the things I would rather forget are still there, locked away in some recess of my being. Every word I have uttered, every deed I have done, every emotion I have felt or expressed, and all that was done or said to me, *everything* is wrapped up in that entity called me.

I may not like some of it — I want to get on top of some aspects of my past and control or release facets of my present character — but that is work for tomorrow. Today, I acknowledge and accept all that has gone before as my experience of life.

I know I have within me the potential to be anything I want to be. From within, I can create the person I want to be.

I want to be loving, strong, radiant. Yet I feel I am nowhere near that now. But I know these qualities are within my reach. They are inside me. I simply have not yet tapped them.

I want to be successful and to win the respect and recognition of others. Those goals are within reach. I can stir up from my very core the drive and the determination it takes to achieve those goals.

I am raw material at my disposal to shape into what I choose to make of myself. The kind of person I am and the kinds of things I do are entirely up to me.

I have the capacity in me to become anything. I can be a successful, kind, loving, generous person. The ugly truth is also that I could be a cold miser, a penniless drunk, a road-rage brawler. The potential for wretchedness and evil lurks within me.

So I can't be scornful of my brothers and sisters who are the wretched of the earth. I can hate their behavior, yes. But I don't look at them as some lower form of beings to be loathed, because I am only a string of bad choices away from being the same thing.

I look at every person I may tend to detest —
from the murderer to the drug addict who
sleeps on filthy streets — and say, "There,
but for the grace of God, go I." In doing so, I
uncover my compassion and forgiveness.
Also, I pay tribute to myself and my choices
in life.

Like those who followed the path to self-
destruction, I, too, was at that crossroads:
thoughts of doing harm to another have
flashed through my mind; thoughts of giving
up on my moral values have tempted me; the
desire to turn coldly away from the world has
presented itself to me.

But I have had the presence of mind, the
strength and the grace of God with me that I
have been able to dismiss those thoughts and
desires. Just think, if I had acted on them,
how my life would have been sucked into a
vortex of wretchedness.

It boils down to this: choice. I can be evil, hate-filled, destructive. I can be good, loving, constructive. I recognize my potential to be anything, even if that means admitting I can be a hateful person.

I congratulate myself on the choices I have already made. And I make further choices to be the best, most wonderful, loving and lovable person I can be.

So many people go through life acquiring personality traits and adopting habits without taking time to assess them. Now is the time for me to stop and take a long, honest look at myself.

Am I all that I want to be? In answering, I won't think of what anyone else wanted me to be or told me I could never be. I will think only of myself, of my likes and dislikes and of the kind of person I will be happy being.

In creating the me I want to be, I will think of people I admire. What is it about them that I would like to emulate and adapt to myself and my situation? And I will think of those I don't admire. What is it that I find unpleasant about them? Do I have those traits and what can I do to rid myself of them?

As I develop a clearer picture of the kind of person I want to be, I will imagine myself daily acting, talking and behaving as that person. When I wake up in the morning and before I go to bed, I will conjure up a mental image of that kind, loving, honest, unselfish me. When I look in the mirror, I will see that wonderful me reflected in my face. And every day, I will do something tangible to bring that person into being — say the words I imagine the new me would say, make the actions I imagine the new me would make.

I am a creature of emotions. I have the capacity to feel love, anger, joy, sorrow, bitterness, tenderness, embarrassment, pride, arrogance, sympathy, scorn, triumph, glee.

I love and revel in the emotions that make me feel good about myself, others and the world. But I could do without the anger and pain and every other emotion that makes me think less of myself, others and the world. Yet I know I will experience the gamut of emotions, the good, yes, but the bad and the ugly ones as well: there's no escaping it. Life is just like that.

Emotions are an essential part of what it means to be human. To experience emotions fully is to feel fully alive. When feelings come, I will try to let them run their reasonable course through me. I'll cry out the tears, beat my pillow in anger, laugh from deep within my belly, jump and whoop and dance for joy.

But all things — good and bad — must come to an end.

If anger persists for days and I find I feel no joy when the warmth of the sun is on my face, then the anger has usurped the throne of my heart; it is no longer in its reasonable place in my life. The same is true of joy. If I am so blissful about meeting someone that I let this happiness prevent me from feeling the anger I should feel at his or her maltreatment of me or others, then that joy is no longer in its reasonable place.

The longer I live, the more I realize I must
not let my emotions run amok in me. When
they threaten to overrun my life and predomi-
nate in an unreasonable way or paralyze me,
it is time for me to take control. I must be the
one ultimately in charge.

People around me have a big impact on my life. I need people. I want their admiration, their approval. I want people, especially those I love most, to be proud of me.

But I am growing to realize that their opinions are secondary to my own. This is my life, not theirs.

So when I make choices, I consider their expectations and advice, certainly. But I now have the strength to discard all that others say and focus on my expectations of myself. I have caused myself enough pain by living according to what I believed others expected of me. Now I will consider above all else what would make me feel I have made the best use possible of this time on earth with which I have been blessed. This is all that counts in the end.

I listen to the voices that speak silently inside. What do they say? I had long thought it was me carrying on a dialogue with myself. But often it is not. The voices I hear often do not belong to me. They belong to my parents, brothers, sister, relatives, teachers, school-mates, neighbors, boss, co-workers, strangers on the street, some imaginary "they". They all tell me what to think, what to do, what is expected of me. Mostly, they whip me and inhibit me. They have driven me to do things that make me feel dissatisfied with myself. They have told me to refrain from doing things I want to do because they say to do so would be selfish.

I listen to these voices. I consider their perspective. But no longer will I blindly obey. I will search for my own answers. And I will fight those voices with an argument of my own. Those voices are already beginning to subside and be replaced by my own as I do the work of finding and loving myself.

I never have all the answers to all my questions. I never have that sense of certainty about my life and about my choices which I thought would have come naturally with adulthood. And that often leaves me with a sense of confusion and frustration.

But I will rise above these sinking feelings. I will lift my head up and continue to seek answers. I will look around at all possibilities. I know from past experience that I am often surprised at how many routes forward I find once I start looking. I ask only for divine guidance so I can make the best choice of all the possibilities available to me.

In whatever I do, I will ask myself this: "Is this the best way for me to spend this minute?" Each minute is precious. I can never tell when the hands of time will stop for me.

I strive to be good, but sometimes I am so vexed by a situation I do or say things to hurt someone. I try to lead a life of serenity, but there are days when I scream and shout and behave unreasonably. I am not perfect and neither am I consistent.

I am learning to feel no shame or guilt about this. I am human. It is the same with nature. Nature is neither consistent nor perfect: the sun does not rise or set in the same spot every day; the trees never have the same number of leaves; the banks of the river may seem the same, but they are continuously being eroded. So I accept my inconsistencies; I forgive myself for my imperfections, even as I strive to be the best me that I can be.

Journey

to

Joy

———

When I am in a situation that causes me pain, I will do something about it. Search for solutions. Try something different. Make a move. Experiment.

To stay in the painful situation and simply hope it gets better is to subject myself to needless torture. A change will happen only when I make it.

After sorrow comes joy. After mourning there is dancing again.

But happiness will not return on its own. It's up to me to claim my new joy. I have to leave my dark mourning chamber and step out into the sunshine of a new day.

So, what is it that's robbing me of my joy? I
will investigate. I will search deep inside to
find the source of my constant displeasure. I
need to size it up. Am I being rational to
mope about it? What can I do to correct the
situation? Is it something I can't change,
must accept and must leave behind?

I will do the work now instead of letting that
which ails me fester inside and sour my life. I
can rid myself of that canker and give myself
the chance to breathe lightly and smile easily.
I will conquer those things that silently eat
away at my happiness. It is not my lot in life
to move through all my days with a heavy
heart and weariness written all over my face.

The cure for misery is to remove myself from
those things that make me miserable and to
fill my days with the things that bring me joy.

When worry plagues me, I know it is a false affliction; the problem is simply that I am looking at life from an unhelpful vantage point. If I stop staring at the cloud that hovers in front of me, if I look in another direction, I will see brilliant sunshine.

Worry is magnifying unpleasant possible outcomes. It is unreal because the future is not yet made. No matter how hopeless my prospects may seem, I may encounter some magic that can transform my situation. Any miracle could happen to me today.

When I worry, I choose the worst outcome. I claim it by focusing on it, by letting it reign in my thoughts. And because I project it into my future reality, chances are the things I do or fail to do will bring the unpleasant outcome into being.

Life is sweeter when I banish worry, when I choose optimism instead. This is as equally unreal as worry since optimism is a projection of the best outcome, which, of course, has not yet come to pass. But how much more relaxed and pleasant my days are when I choose to base them on positive projection rather than squander them in worry. It is when I expect a bright future for myself that I perk up and move forward to greet it. And in doing so, I make actions and set in motion events that will indeed bring me a brighter future.

I am bombarded continuously with negatives. From the lips of others to the cracks in the ceiling, there are myriad sources telegraphing messages that could sink my soul under the weight of their negativity.

I don't have to give in to their pressure. In fact, I will borrow strategy from them to fight them effectively. The negatives are prevalent, pervasive. I run into them often and almost everywhere I turn.

Well, I will take control of my environment. I will turn it into one pulsating with positiveness. I will fill it with beauty that will gladden my eyes and nourish my soul. I will plaster my environment with positive sayings that will fill me up and give me a boost at every turn. I will banish the words and songs that pull me down. Instead, I will fill my ears with words and music that enrich me and lift me up.

Moods are infectious. I notice this when I am watching a movie. The hero crumples in tears as his beloved gasps her final breath, and I, too, burst into tears. I experience it in daily life. The waiter is surly when taking my order and I vow not to leave a tip.

The mood I carry around with me will be transferred to those I come into contact with — and will be reflected back to me. So what is my mood? Is it angry? Is it bitter? Is it self-pitying? These may get me a place among certain old biddies who like to huddle together and gossip, or among barflies whose only recreation is putting down every person they've had the misfortune to meet. But if I want love and joy in my life, these moods will do me no good. I will carry, instead, a cheerful spirit each time I step out of my front door. I know that every time I've ever done so, the world has returned that joy to me.

Gloominess can attack my thoughts. It will present itself on my face. What is my persistent facial expression, the one I carry when there is no one else around? Glum? Frowning? Worried? It's time to crack that grim mask. Replace it with an exaggerated expression of joy.

I will smile, even if I don't feel like it. Spread those lips wide apart. Stretch my facial muscles. Or even better, open my mouth and laugh scandalously, as if I have just heard the best joke ever.

I will let my entire body express joy — walk with a skip in my step, dance, applaud the sunrise, hug myself. My mental outlook and feelings will follow my physical expression.

Being a happy person is a choice. Just as I decide what clothes to wear, I can choose what mood to wear. The more often I choose to wear one of cheerfulness, the more it becomes part of me. As I fight this persistent gloom, I am finding that I am choosing to smile or adopt a light-hearted approach, even when the going gets rough. So I will be more deliberate in this. I will throw sourness, bitterness, hate and all other negatives out of my mood closet. I will dress myself daily with joy, laughter, sweetness. Life is too short for me to do otherwise.

I choose life. I choose happiness. Life is exciting, full of promise and joy. I open my heart and mind to it.

Laughter and joy are dangling in the air around me. I will grab hold of them. I will make them part of my life.

When I realize I am wallowing in bitterness for too long, I will force myself to do joyful things — take a walk in the woods and listen to the wind in the leaves; treat myself to a long, lazy sun-bath on a summer afternoon; read a book of jokes.

There are millions of healthy, helpful things I can do to add sweetness to my days. I will choose these.

I will make time to do things that please me.
I will use a portion of each day to engross
myself in activities that have nothing to do
with earning a living, taking care of responsi-
bilities or satisfying duties to others. I will
take that "me time" religiously. I deserve it. It
is my life. I have a right to enjoy it.

I have a choice. I can live my life in a cocoon. In such a world, everything is simple and easy because everything is familiar. I enclose myself in a tight, small space of known experiences that I repeat.

My other choice is to live in the wide, open world. I can take myself into experiences that are new and challenging. I can flutter about several corners of the garden, even if I have a particular shady spot that I return to.

Life is short. My days are limited. The opportunity to live and experience is fleeting and much too good to be wasted in the confines of a cocoon.

I will open up to the world. I will let people into my life. Not indiscriminately, no: but I will be open to all; embrace many; allow the privilege of intimacy to only those who prove themselves worthy.

The more open I am, the less stressed I will be because I will no longer feel the need to defend my borders all the time. The more acquaintances and friends I have, the more resources and help are available to me. And in turn, the more open I am to the world, the more I have the opportunity to share of myself and to be a help to someone else in need.

When I am at my lowest ebb, like I am today, I will remind myself that I am not alone in having to endure struggles. Others have had and are now having failures, heartaches and disappointments. Others have had and are having worse troubles piled upon their heads. That does not make my burdens any less. But it is comforting to remember this because it makes me realize I have not been singled out for special torture. The cry "Why me?" becomes irrelevant; it flees and I have one less source of pain.

Blue days are part of life. When they come, I
will not torture myself by thinking they will
last forever. They, too, will pass. I will experience them and move on. There is no need to
fear them or to reproach myself with the
thought that I have failed to get everything
right with my life. I will get through them
and keep moving. Keep moving on.

Often when I am being crushed under the weight of my difficulties, I fool myself into believing one day I will be over all troubles and heartaches. But the "problem-free future" in this life is a lie. The future will not be total bliss, just as the past has not been and the present is not.

I accept that I will always have to deal with difficulties. I will even try to look forward to this. I can only win if I see every difficulty as a game, and if I take it on for the challenge and pleasure of seeing how well I can play.

Whatever problem I face, how well or how quickly I come through it depends mostly on how I look at the situation and how I feel. Positive thoughts and positive feelings turn the problem into a challenge, one I have a better chance of overcoming because of my bright attitude. Also, the experience of taking on the challenge will be an enriching, rather than a soul-sapping one.

I must take things easy. Take things light.
Cool down. Calm my future-fears. Work
hard, yes. But live and enjoy.

Why do I have to endure so much pain? I ask this question over and over again. But I know I should stop complaining about the suffering. I need to embrace it. Deal with it. That's life. Pain tests you, improves you. Anybody can be happy in good times, but to experience pain and be happy in spite of it means you have learnt to live.

Wisdom and understanding bring freedom
from the pain that foolish mistakes cost me.
And yet, wisdom and understanding often
can be gained only through the pain caused
by foolish mistakes.

It is not only the triumphs that bring growth
or are a sign of progress. The failures, too,
teach me to grow. How I handle them shows
how well I have learnt to live.

Learning and living; the words are almost synonyms. Each day brings new experiences and new opportunities to learn. Some lessons are quick and easy. Others are drawn-out and painful. I will take them both with a good spirit. I will look for the lessons in each experience. I will try to remember the lessons I've learnt along the way and let them guide me as I encounter new opportunities to learn.

I will congratulate myself on my every achievement. It may be a tiny matter, but I will recognize the way in which I have progressed. When I have learnt yet one more thing on this journey of life, I will reward myself with praise, with a smile, a dance or some kind of favorite treat.

This experience called life is going to end one day for me. There will come a time when I will no longer have the ability to see the sun rise or to smell a puppy's breath. It will happen, this inevitability called death.

So I cherish my days. I will be thankful for all my experiences — yes, even the ugly, brutal and painful ones. The thrilling and the tasking experiences all come together to make up my life. I would be ripping myself off if I were to say, "I hate my life now. I'm waiting for that calm time of perfect happiness to enjoy life." Such a phase does not exist in this life.

I will live this day, and love this day. I experience its pains and open up myself to its joys, for the opportunity to laugh is open to me even in the gloomiest moment. I honor each and every day God grants me. It may be my last.

Living is not something I can put off. I may want to say, "I'll dedicate myself to studying now and enjoy life when I graduate," or, "I've got to throw myself into becoming rich and when I succeed, I'll be able to do all the fun things I wanted," or, "When I retire, I'll begin to really live." That is folly.

Even if I think I have suspended my life as I pursue my goals, this is not true. I am still living and shaping myself. The quality of my life during my pursuit will form character, attitudes, habits. If I make the pursuit of my goals everything and neglect a balanced life, then that existence is of a poor quality and can threaten my enjoyment of the very things I seek.

To accomplish anything, dedication to the goal and devotion of time, thought and effort are needed. This is a principle that can not be changed. But what I must learn to do is to make achieving goals part of the bigger package of my experience of life — which should also include goodies like loving, sharing, playing, growing. If achieving a goal is the only thing in the package, I am robbing myself of the fullness of life.

Time wasted can never be regained. Opportunities lost are gone for good. I must live life fully now.

It is said a journey of 1,000 miles begins with one footstep. That is true. Often you set out and the destination is nowhere in sight. But you know you won't get there if you don't take that first step.

It is also true that a journey of 1,000 miles is made up of millions of steps. To get there you must cover every single inch of those 1,000 miles. You can not do that instantly or all at once. You have to do it bit by bit, over time.

I must enjoy the effort and the time it takes to get from here to there. I may make the best of plans and set down a reasonable travel schedule. But the unexpected may happen to upset my itinerary. If I were to tell myself, "I'll wait for my arrival at my destination and then I'll be happy," I will be condemning myself never to enjoy my journey. That is not to say I may never reach where I intend to go. I very well may, even faster than I expected. But if I look to the last inch of my 1,000 miles to be everything, then I will miss the beauty and pleasures of the distances in between my outset and destination.

I realize now that what matters is not the final arrival itself but *me and how I travel* each inch of those 1,000 miles. If I have traveled well, I will arrive refreshed and happy, and my destination will simply be the first step of yet another happy journey. If I have blocked myself off from the pleasures along the way, looking to the journey's end for happiness, I will arrive empty, angry and with so many expectations that I can not but be disappointed.

I am going to exit this world one day. I remind myself of that certainty continually. Each morning, I will thank God for blessing me with another day. Each night, I will thank God for having allowed me to make it through that day. I will ever be aware that the time will come when I will not be able to say either prayer.

Life is exciting. I open up myself to its electricity. I put myself in the stream of its pulsating vibrations.

It's a gift, this ability to breathe, to see, to do. I will make full use of the opportunity. I have only one chance to live any given moment of my life.

It's wonderful to wake up in the morning. I feel excited over this apparent "nothing". I feel joy just because I am alive.

The
Purposeful
Journey

My thoughts can be the source of my power
or my pain. I can determine what they will
be. I can leave my mind open and let
whatever ideas which want to occupy my
mind take up residence there. Or I can police
those thoughts.

I have the right to stop thoughts at the door
of my mind. If they will be unhelpful — if
they are just the same old, depressing,
pain-bearing, soul-dampening, go-nowhere
thoughts I have entertained before — I owe it
to myself to shut the door on them.

I have an obligation to myself to invite soul-
enriching, self-building, life-enhancing
thoughts to dance across the stage of my
mind. It is my mind. It is mine to control.

I will wrestle with my thoughts. I will be in charge of my behavior. I will live consciously instead of letting life happen to me.

I will visualize my future; I will create the me I want to be inside and then go about the job of bringing that person into the world.

My nature and my nurturing have thrown obstacles in my path. But there are literally millions of people who don't let either the circumstances of their birth or their upbringing stop them from realizing the vision they have of themselves: the sickly girl who grew up to be a gold-winning Olympian; the men and women who knew only abject poverty, yet now control million-dollar enterprises; the boy who was put in the class for idiots and later became a doctor; the woman who grew up in a home of bitterness and fighting and yet turned into a loving mother and supportive wife.

I have within me the capacity to be more of what I am today or the opposite of what I am today. Characteristics I lack, I can incorporate and develop. Those aspects of myself I do not like, I can acknowledge and put under tight reins.

My behavior is entirely under my control.
Yes, the situation I was born into and the
conditioning from my environment do
determine my *inclination* to act in certain
ways. But I am a victim of these
circumstances only if I allow myself to be.

I can spot a confident person from a mile away. People who value themselves and have faith in their abilities walk briskly, with a sense of purpose. They hold their head high. Their shoulders are rolled back. Up close, they are even more impressive. Their handshake is firm and they look you directly in the eyes. They speak up, in a clear, unwavering voice. They don't retreat from people or situations; instead, they move forward to meet others and confront challenges. Hence, they always get noticed and people want to be around them.

Who can fail to admire people with a go-getter attitude? They may be faced with seemingly insurmountable challenges, yet they refuse to act defeated. They are ready to put up a good fight, and they expect to win. They are not ones to cry into their beer and complain to everyone who will spare an ear about what a bad hand life has dealt them. Other people may see a wall blocking their path and abandon their journey, but not these; they see that wall as an opportunity to learn climbing skills and to develop muscles as they continue on their path. And with this attitude, this positive drive, it is no surprise that these people do indeed win in the game of life.

Positiveness and confidence go hand in hand. A positive person says "I can", and a confident person believes those two words to be true.

How does one become one of those bright, cheerful persons whom the world loves and who attract success? Positiveness is an attitude, an approach to life that says there is a solution to every problem.

Some people have the advantage of growing up in a positive environment, where the adults around them rose to the challenges that life threw at them. Others, however, had only the example of whiners and losers who, rather than fight wisely and valiantly, threw the towel in the ring at the first sight of the challenge.

Being positive is a habit, an attitude. And a habit or an attitude is something anyone can adopt at any stage in life. So, even those who were bred in a negative environment can become one of those glowing, vibrant persons who win admiration all around and succeed in life.

Being positive does not mean you minimize or ignore the difficulties of life. It means you face them squarely and say, "Okay, I'll have to make more of an effort than I thought, but I *can* do this."

All great accomplishments in this world
began as thoughts. They first existed as ideas;
they started life simply as the desires of the
doer. Then those ideas were acted upon.

If I want to do anything, I must start the
process in my mind and heart. I will cultivate
dreams. I will become passionate about them.
This is the spark that will ignite my engine
and enable me to achieve great things.

I will dream big. All things are possible. I can achieve any great feat I imagine.

I will dream wisely. I must know the things that are truly important in life. Love is chief among them.

I will dream big with love at the center of my dreams. Success and successful living should go hand-in-hand.

I am working on a plan for my life and I am planning to work that plan. I am giving myself a timetable for each step towards my goals and I will celebrate each achievement along the way. Without a plan, I know I am drifting aimlessly through my days. Working a plan makes the experience of living worthwhile and a lot more interesting.

As I search for direction in life, I will listen
to these words that whisper inside:

> Do what you love. Do what your
> soul tells you you were brought
> into this world to do. Your life has
> a purpose. You were meant to
> accomplish some particular feat or
> feats. This work is meaningful to
> you, deeply satisfying.

What is it? I will search inside and find it.
Life presents me with so many distractions.
But I need to stop for a while and tune out all
outside voices. I need to listen to my own
voice. I need to listen to God's voice. The
answer as to my purpose will come in, crystal
clear. And when I have found it, I won't let
anyone or any circumstance steal it from me.
My life work is my gift to myself, and to the
world. It is the unfolding of my promise; it is
the legacy that says I lived. I will fight for it.
I will struggle with it. I will do that work
which I love, for doing it is its own reward.

Do I know what I want? Am I sure? Am I
clear about the consequences? I must be
certain of what I want. It is the necessary first
step to asking for it and doing what is needed
to bring it into being.

There will be rough days ahead, no matter which road I choose in this life. There is no painless route to take.

I will look as far as I can see down every road before I step onto a path. How rough and risky does each seem? Which paths are dangerous or difficult? Which one will lead me to the destination I desire?

The final question is the most important. Where is it that I want to go in life? The paths may be inviting in themselves. But I will use only one basis to choose a path: not that it is picturesque or seemingly less difficult than the others, but simply because it promises to take me surely to where I want to go.

Success in any endeavor takes hard work.
Many other ingredients are involved —
patience, wisdom, determination, tenacity.
But hard work is perhaps the key factor.

It is the element missing in so many people
who fail. They may not even get off the
ground with their project because they are
daunted by the prospect of putting out so
much effort. Some may get going but fall off
early because they drop the pace. Others
reach far and, sadly, lose the chance to collect
their prize because they give up at the last
moment. But I must not.

Hard work. What is there to fear in that? I
start something, I must give it my all. Push,
push, push and then push some more. What
do I have to lose? If I don't apply myself or
sustain my effort, I risk losing everything. I
have one lifetime in which to accomplish
anything. If I don't put in the hard work now,
when will I achieve?

Seek balance in everything — work, love, pleasures, giving. That is my daily struggle. I want a total experience of life. I want to use all of me, or at least as much of me as it is good and possible to explore.

So I will not use the pursuit of a goal to exclude the pursuit of love. I won't allow concerns after family to extinguish those hobbies that fire my soul. When I shut out all other pursuits to go after my goals, life becomes less interesting and my goals themselves lose their shine. When I give more of myself than I should to others, they become dependent and I feel taken advantage of.

Inside, there is a scale that tells me when things are out of balance. My overall sense of ease will let me know when I need to add more or take away some from any aspect of my life in order to achieve that balance which sustains happiness.

I will have good days and bad days. I accept that. I won't expect to be on a high at all times. I won't be at 100 per cent in my performance for all of my life. Sometimes I may dip below 50 per cent. Often I will surprise myself by exceeding what I thought was my 100 per cent.

I will praise myself fully when I do better than even I expected. I will congratulate myself for maintaining my average. I will refrain from fretting and beating up on myself when I don't perform as well as I could. I will accept it as just part of a cycle, and work towards getting in form again.

Often in my life, I will reach a point where the way ahead is blocked. It may seem as if there is little hope to get beyond the obstacles. But I won't let that hold me back. I know from past experience that once I get up and start seeking, my mind will attract the positives that will show me the way. God will send people and circumstances to guide me. I will open up and receive them.

When in the midst of my darkest hour a little sign of hope comes, I won't hesitate; I will run to it, grab hold of it. I may not be sure exactly where I am heading or what I have in my hands. But I will keep running and holding on, for to chase even a spark of hope is better than to lie paralyzed by despair.

I can deal with an obstacle in any number of ways: climb over it; dig my way under it; go around it; blast my way through it; push it out of my path. Or I may leave that path and, instead, take a detour to my destination. I can even change destinations.

Every problem has a multitude of solutions. I believe I will find one to take me where I want to be.

I can take charge and control many things about my life. But there are many other things over which I am powerless.

When I confront such situations, I will say: "So be it." It was not meant to be as I wanted.

I will trust that God's alternative plan is much better than my own.

Failure and disappointment are the result of reality catching up with my unrealistic expectations.

I can not change reality by ignoring it. I can not wish reality away. Reality is what it is and will be what it will be. I have no choice but to work with it.

Mistakes and unsuccessful outcomes are part of life. There is no need to fear them. An unsuccessful outcome does not make me less of a person. It is a lesson. It warns of yet another pitfall to avoid in order to ensure successful results the next time I try.

Sometimes I will get derailed. Life is not as simple as a straight, one-way track. There are dangerous twists and turns. There are unexpected and seemingly insignificant bends that can take me way off course before I know it.

That is why I must have a clear focus on where I plan to take myself in life. I must know what I want for myself today. I must be clear on what I want for my future, and, always, I must assess what I am doing now. Is it going to take me there?

If the answer is yes, I will happily continue on my course. If it is no, I will acknowledge I've got derailed.

Ah well, it happens. There's no time for blame and self-persecution. I will simply pick myself up and get myself back on track.

I must keep going. The road will become rough in parts. I may find myself stumbling with every step. I may be bruised. I may feel battered. But I will keep going.

The journey may become boring at times. I may look around and the scenery may be just the same old, same old. I will trust that an exciting change is around the bend. And keep going.

I may feel alone sometimes. Others may even be with me at that moment, but I will face the fact that life is a solitary journey. I will embrace that truth. I will embrace myself. And keep going.

I will keep hope ever alive. I will keep ever
reaching for that better day. I will appreciate
today, love the present. Live it fully. And see
a better, brighter, sweeter everything for
myself at the next turn. I expect a better
tomorrow and I will do everything I can
today to make it happen.

Journey

to

Love

———

Hurt no one. Help others. That's my guide. With love at the center of my life, I will develop quality relationships that will make my experience of living enjoyable.

My life is made up of my relationships: with myself, with God, with others, with material things, with natural things. I will place love at the center of all these relationships.

We are all connected. The hurt and joy, the pain and freedom, the laughter and tears that originate from any one of us flow into the big, invisible pool in which we all live, fouling or sweetening it. If I say angry words to someone, that person is likely to carry his bitterness into his next encounter. If I make someone smile, that person is likely to be cheerful with the next person she meets. What will be my contribution to the energy pool of life today?

In my lifetime, I will have encounters with hundreds of people, many of whom will disappoint me and do things — intentionally or otherwise — to hurt me.

I must forgive them all their trespasses. They, too, are only human. They, too, like me, are facing struggles. So, I must be kind to others. By no means let them take advantage of me. I must stand up for myself. I owe it to myself to defend myself when the situation calls for it. But I must do so without malice. I must leave an ugly situation without ugliness in my thoughts and heart. These others do not have the answers, cocky as they may appear. In fact, the more arrogant and vindictive they are, the further they are from truth, self-knowledge and self-love. They have a long journey to get there. My duty is to forgive them for their hurts against me and wish them well on their journey.

Not everyone will like me. There are those who will hate me although I have done nothing to deserve their contempt. It could be prejudice or envy or some other form of ugliness in their heart that blocks openness and acceptance.

I must watch for such obstacles to love in myself. I strive to keep love vibrant in my life, to love everyone, even the most heinous. It's something I have to *do*, not just contemplate as a desirable way to live. So, I must look at everyone and *choose* to see the good in them, focus on the tiny piece of God they carry within them. I will love them and wish them well on their journey of life. And I will demonstrate my love to as many as I can — by lending a hand, sharing a smile, giving of what I possess, showing concern, caring.

Do I, see color or race when I am among others? Color-blindness is a wonderful, richly rewarding virtue to have. How magnificent it is to be with another person and see only personality, not tint of epidermis or texture of hair; to be free of notions of what that person should be — stupid, aggressive, venal, insincere, weak, intelligent — because of the history of his or her ancestors; to see only what choices this human being before me has made as to how to use this precious opportunity to live.

In the end, what matters more than the type of vessel a person inhabits or the environment in which that vessel was dented or polished, is what's inside the vessel.

Jesus advised us to treat others as we would
have them treat us. I would not want anyone
to hurt me, to lie to me, to cheat me, betray
me, steal what is mine, abandon me,
disrespect me or humiliate me. So I must not
do it to others.

Of course, not everyone lives by this rule. So
other people do hurt me, and betray me, and
humiliate me. And no, it isn't fair. So how do
I respond? Should I even the score? Do I give
them back a bit of just what they are dishing
out?

Well that would be operating by their rules,
wouldn't it? That would be turning my back
on my own principles. I might as well not
have principles in the first place if I allow
other people's actions to determine my
behavior.

So what do I do when others treat me badly and the temptation is strong to treat them roughly in return? Someone slaps me on one side of the face and I itch to strike him down. I must refuse to let his behavior lead mine. I would prefer someone not hit me. So instead of striking back, I must turn the other cheek.

Some things are worth fighting for, but losses
are a foregone conclusion in some battles and
those should never be entered into. For
instance, when someone is involved in self-
destructive behavior, you can never rescue
that person. You can plead. You can beg. You
can reason and advise until your throat runs
dry. You will still never succeed in changing
that person.

The will to change comes from within. How
can I kick-start that will in someone else? I
can't. It is only when the person hits a low
and realizes his behavior will lead to his ruin
that he will change — if he wants to save
himself.

Instead of wasting my energy in the futile
fight to rescue another, I will seek to rescue
myself — I have enough work as it is to
make me a better person.

Sometimes, I may unintentionally bring pain to someone through well-meaning enthusiasm or through ignorance. Often in such a case, my absence of malice puts me on the defensive and it becomes a matter of pride to deny having done wrong or caused hurt. That only makes matters worse.

I know what my experience of a situation is. I must open up and realize that others, seeing the same situation through different eyes and feeling it with different skin, may have a completely different experience to my own. I will open up and see life through the eyes of others, feel it through their skin.

When someone tells me I have done damage, as humbling as it may be to have to do so, I must acknowledge his or her hurt and say I am sorry. And I need to make the reparations I would have asked for if I had been the one who had been hurt.

People will anger me, disturb me, disappoint me. I may find them ugly, stupid, boring, insensitive. But the reality is, I need people.

I need to be warmed by the energy that flows when two human beings are together. For I know that even if it's a simple, short encounter, when I am with someone else, sparks fly and some facet of my being is enlivened, ignited. And, strangely, this is true even if the encounter is a negative one.

Solitude is necessary to refresh myself, to recharge my batteries, to discover my inner world. But solitude is good for a certain length of time only. When I have done the internal work that solitude allows me to do, it is essential that I get back into the stream of life. I need to mix and mingle with others, to share my life force with them and to receive of their life force.

I will cherish and be grateful for little things
that seem like nothing, but which actually
mean a lot — like having family and true
friends to turn to. Those same people with
whom I have quarreled and shed tears and
shared laughter, they are priceless. During my
crisis, they may not be able to give me anything tangible to help me out of my hole. But
at least I know they will be around to hear
my cries for help. Even if miles separate us,
remembering them lets me know I am not
alone. I am loved. Even if the rest of the
world seems unwelcoming, I am known and
loved by these important few.

I always thought I needed to appear strong,
but now I've learnt the important lesson that
when I need help, I can reach out for it.
When I feel tired, I can look for a friendly
shoulder to rest my head upon. A burden
shared is a burden lightened.

There is no shame in feeling weak, lost, confused. I am human. I won't always be strong and in control. There is no harm in letting those I love and who love me know of the times when I am at my lowest point.

Sure, it's nice to prove myself to them; it's wonderful to have those I love feel proud of me and look up to me. But now I know that those who love me truly will never look down on me for being human and imperfect. Instead, they feel closer to me, love me more deeply and give me strength because I opened up to them — because I needed them.

I must *be* love.

I must take the time and make the effort to be
there for those who may need me, just as in
the past I needed others to be there for me —
and I will need them in the future.

There are often times when I am hurting and all I need is a hug and to know someone cares. Others feel the same way too. Others need me.

It takes a certain amount of courage to reach out to others. I am sometimes shy to open up to others because they may reject my approaches. It may turn out that they want more of me than I can give. I may discover they are not the kind of people with whom I'd like to continue to be associated.

But I must be brave. I will risk rejection. I will risk making a connection from which I may have to pull away later. But I may find there was no risk at all in reaching out to others. What I may discover, instead, is a wonderful person who was scared to reach out to me and ask for help because he or she was similarly fearful of imagined risks.

I will do little acts of kindness for others.
Help another, without waiting to be asked.
Give and share and spread love and joy to
others. I know the love and joy will come
back to me.

I am a light that shines eternally. I will turn
up the power and be a beacon wherever there
is darkness.

Human beings are human beings; there is no
one greater or lesser than me. In spite of the
greatest achievement a woman has had or the
lowliest act a man has committed, every one
is still, like me, a mass of flesh with blood
coursing through their veins and with an
inner world, a soul, which they may or may
not acknowledge. Like me, they are on a
journey. They may be confused or confident,
weak or resilient, enlightened or ignorant as
they follow their course in life. Howsoever it
may be with them, I will ever remember that
big or small in wealth, power, fame, educa-
tion or experience, each and every person I
see will at some future date cease to exist,
just like I will. And howsoever that other
person may be, each second of his or her life
is as precious as every second of mine.

The
Spiritual
Journey

———

I am wonderful and worthy of love and all good things just because I exist. God made me. I am special just because I am here. I am unique, precious. God allowed me to enter this world because *I was meant to be.*

How great and wonderful it is to be free of burdens, liberated from worries and cares. That liberty is always available to me. God is always there with a ready hand to lift the burdens from my shoulders. I can't throw them off alone. Loaded down by their weight, I don't have the strength to throw them off by myself. I will call for help when I need it. What a comfort it is to know that God is always ready to respond to my call.

In everything I do, I will follow my conscience. There is an internal guiding light, a gift from God, that will lead me onto the right path. The distractions of the world threaten to snuff out this light. That is why I need quiet time every day to shut out the world and rekindle my inner flame.

I will feed my soul. Like every living thing, my soul needs care and nurturing. It needs to be a healthy and strong part of my life in order to give me back strength in my most wretched moments.

My soul wants to be recognized. My soul wants its importance to be acknowledged. My soul wants its presence to be appreciated. When it gets none of this attention my soul becomes stifled, buried under my burdens. When I ignore my soul, it's no wonder I feel hollow and impoverished inside. And when the hard times hit, it's no wonder I crumble completely; I have stifled the very thing I needed to shore me up.

I will take some quiet time every day to pay homage to my inner self. At the start of the day, at its end, I will ensure I shut out all the stimuli of the world. I will be there in the quiet to recognize my soul. Acknowledge it. Appreciate its presence.

I am a child of God. I need divine guidance in life. Sure, there's a lot I can learn on my own and from others. But there is much I can never know and will never be able to do without help from my spiritual source.

I will return to the source for refreshment, for sustenance, for strength. I look to the source of my life for a more abundant life. I surrender to the source to have victory. I will be guided by the source. I will let the higher power lead me home.

Inside me is an energy that gives me life —
my spirit, my tiny piece of God. That spirit is
not going to occupy this body forever. One
day its service in this body will come to an
end. The lights inside will be switched off.

That day is inevitable. The date is uncertain.
It could be 20, 50, even 83 years from now. It
could be tomorrow. It could be today, within
the next hour. I will treasure this experience
of life while I still have it.

On this side of life I will always have unanswered questions about God. It is impossible to know everything I want to know with absolute certainty or to get hard, scientific proof about matters concerning God. And are there ever major questions! Does God really exist? And if God exists, in what form? Which doctrine among the many to choose from represents the true voice of God? What does God expect of me? And if I die without fulfilling those expectations, what will happen to me?

Those who say they've found God still don't have all the answers. It is possible to love God and follow a course that you believe would please God. But God and matters of the spirit are huge and perhaps beyond our comprehension. For us mortals of finite minds, God is a mystery. And this is why faith is needed.

I don't know for sure the answers to many of
the questions concerning God and that leaves
me with a choice — either I let that
uncertainty feed disbelief and I disregard the
notion of God, or I accept, with faith, that
God exists and I live a life that my faith tells
me would please God.

At the end of my journey of life, all of this
may not matter at all. Or it may count for
everything.

God is in me. I am in God. God is in everyone else. Everyone else is in God. Through
God, I am connected to all of life, all of those
who came before, who are today and who are
yet to come.

As I awaken my spiritual self and live
through the spirit, I find the notion of
loneliness dissolving from my life. My spirit
is one with God. I am one with God. I am
never alone. The creator of all life, who put
the stars in the sky and the fish in the ocean
and who makes the trees grow, is always with
me.

The golden pathway to joy is gratitude to God. Gratitude brings a sense of peace, humility, love and reassurance. Gratitude to God helps me focus on the things in life that matter the most.

My expectations may come crashing down around me, but if I focus on the things for which I should be grateful to God, all dreadful circumstances lose their sting and no difficulty, how ever great, is able to defeat me. I've lost a dream of love, yet I thank God for granting me good health. My career plans have not gone as I expected, yet I praise God for the love of my family and friends. My hopes in many areas have not come to fruition, yet I bless the Creator that I am still able to listen to the birds and to see the sun rise. God has preserved my life, and therefore hope and joy are mine.

Today may not be perfect, but when I look around, I find God has given me a multitude of reasons to celebrate.

Would you like to contribute to Celia Sankar's next book?
This book will gather the stories of people, both famous and
unknown, who have triumphed over adversity.

At some point in our lives, each of us is struck down by pain and
loss that threaten our very existence. The tragedy is that in those
moments of agony, many feel utterly alone and ashamed: they
think there is something horribly wrong with them because they
can not cope and they despise themselves for the weakness they
feel.

People suffering needlessly in this way can find comfort from
realizing they are not alone, that others, too, have felt knocked
down and beaten up by life. They can have hope from knowing
that others have fought their way back to happy, healthy lives.
And they can become empowered to fight their own battles by
learning what others did to move on to a life of well-being and
joy. Sankar's next book aims to provide that comfort and hope.

You can contribute by sending your story, which should answer
the following questions:
What was the most difficult experience of your life?
How did you respond to it?
How long did this period last?
What did you do to get beyond your difficulty?
How did the words and actions of others affect you during and
after this period?
What lessons have you learnt from this experience?

Send your story to:
Book Contribution
c/o Damascus Press
Suite 201
95 Hutchison Avenue
Elliot Lake, Ontario
Canada P5A 1W9

or to:
info@celiasankar.com

Thank you in advance for sharing your experiences. By doing so,
you are helping others along on their journey.

Share the journey
and the joy with others

To order by phone in the United States or Canada,
call toll free at:
1-800-259-0319
Please have your Visa, Mastercard or American Express
credit card number and expiration date ready.

*We offer a very attractive discount for orders of five
or more copies. Call or write for details.*

Journey to Joy ISBN 0-9689109-1-2 Can$19.95 US$12.95

ORDER FORM

Payable in Canadian or US funds only. Book price: Can$19.95/
US$12.95. Shipping & handling: Can$6/US$4 per book. We
accept Visa, Mastercard and AmEx, checks ($15 fee for returned
checks) and money orders payable to Damascus Press.

Call 1-800-259-0319, fax (705) 848-2828 or mail orders to:

Damascus Press   Credit card#_____
Suite 201   Expiration date _____
95 Hutchison Avenue   ☐ Visa ☐ Mastercard ☐ AmEx
Elliot Lake, Ontario
Canada P5A 1W9   Signature _____

Bill to:_____
Address:_____
City:_____ Prov/St:_____ ZIP:_____
Ship to:_____
Address:_____
City:_____ Prov/St:_____ ZIP:_____
No. copies:_____ Book Total: $ _____
Shipping & handling: $ _____
Total amount due: $ _____

Please allow 4-6 weeks for delivery in Canada.
For US and international orders, please allow 6-8 weeks.
This offer is subject to change without notice.